Dedication

I0409593

This piece of work is dedicated to **Freedom**, to those who have it and for those who fight to obtain it. To people of color who have long to understand how it would feel to be free. To hitchhike across America with no worries, to cycle through Europe in search of oneself. The simplest thing given to all living things, **Freedom**.

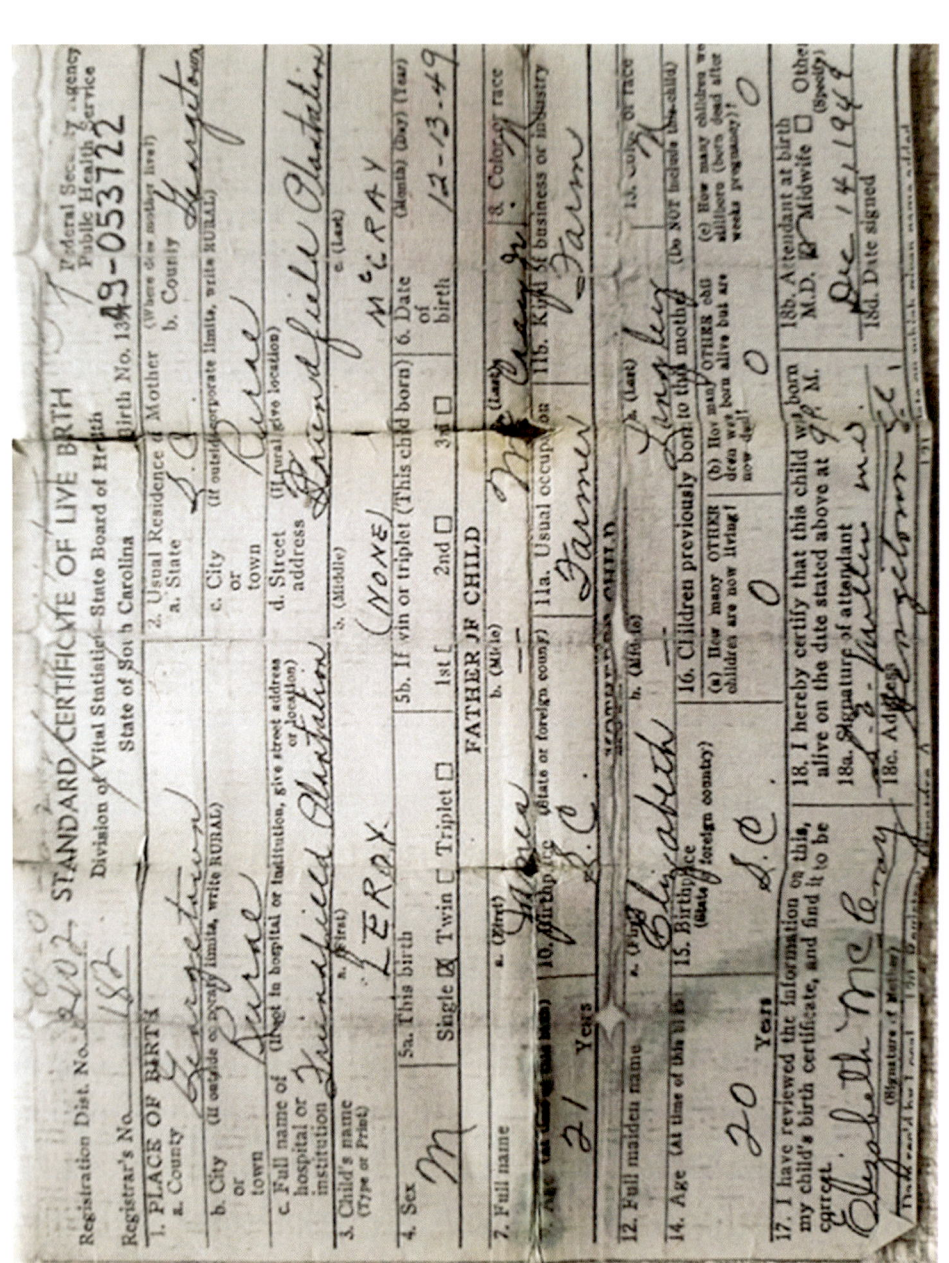

Birth Certificate from 1949

In My Shoes

The word "Plantation" speaks volumes of racism to African Americans and people of color throughout the Americas. This was my beginning, Negroes in Georgetown South Carolina had no hospital. The doctor would come to the plantation just as a vet would come to take care of the animals. I was circumcised at age 3, I can still fill the pain from trying to pee in the pot at my grandmother's house. Now during regular days, I would just be a normal little black child on the plantation, playing with the owner's two children a boy and a little girl which were about a year to two years older than I. I remember the day we went fishing, there was a pond in front of the big house. My father had just brought me a red and blue plastic fishing rod with a large plastic hook. For some reason the young master grabbed my toy rod and said "Niggers can't fish!" as he threw it into the water. I was about 5 years old at this point and not realizing the possible consequences of my actions I pushed him in the water after it. I later realized I was wrong, as my mother was cutting her a willow switch. My mother had gone blind the year before and I still tell people until you get a whipping by a blind black mother you ain't had nothing. But it seems the young man told everyone that he fell in the pond. Which probably saved my life. My time in the south was short lived. My father like most Black men of his time wanted better for himself and his family. The owner of the plantation was also connected to the zoo in Philadelphia, Pa. he got my father employment there and at age 7 which was 1957 we moved to Philadelphia. I remember my father enrolling me in Blaine Elementary School. The White lady informed him that the school systems in the south are a lot behind when it comes to education compared to those in the north. They would have to put me in a lower grade to catch up with the rest of the kids. I couldn't help but think to myself, "Wow two plus two is different up north." There was no test given to evaluate my level of education. However, he agreed him having only a seventh grade education himself. Later that semester we moved and I was transfered to Reynolds Elementary in the heart of the Black community were I started third grade. We had moved over a second hand furniture shop were the building was owned by a Mr. Groin, an elderly Jewish gentleman. After approximately a year of living there with little or no heat Mr. Groin started to furnish a little more coal for the furnace and ask that I learn how to control it, this would be good for me to learn. I became very good at it and before long he asked if I could help him in the store. He had an old station wagon that we would use to go out and collect his goods. We would go into the White neighborhoods to buy or just find items in the trash. When at someone's home I was often told to remain in the car, even though I could see the pointing and the whispers. He would then take these items back to the community, where he would refurbish them in rear of the store and then put them up for sale. He started me off at $0.50 cents a day, which was pretty good for a nine year old. The following year I started on the school bus, going to New Jersey picking. There was a White guy that would take Black workers to Jersey to pick fruits and vegetables. We would catch the bus at 4:00am, because of school I could only go on Saturdays. Being such a little guy I was limited to things like, blueberries, tomatoes, beans etc. I remember the man saying, "Nigga you gotta pick faster than that, to come back." I came back. The little money I made was to help my family, my father was working side jobs to make ends meet.

What's that old saying, "Time sure flies when your having fun." I was twelve years old. My name sake and great uncle had passed and my father and I returned south. It was Saturday after the funeral when everyone decided to, let's go to the beach. Grandma had prepared a great lunch. Then I noticed the men of the family were loading guns. As we prepared for a great day at the beach, the guns were loaded in the trunks of the cars. When we arrived at the beach my eyes beheld one of the strangest things I have ever seen. There was a chainlink fence dividing the beach and running out in the Atlantic ocean. This was to separate the Whites from the Blacks. At twelve years old I couldn't help but notice the water was moving on both sides. The water didn't care what color you were. I later came to understand this was happening throughout the country. The day went well with not so much as a police insight.

The day was coming to an end and we packed up and headed for home. On the way we stopped for some gas. My grandfather gave me a quarter $0.25 cents. I proceeded in the station, were I purchased a honey bun which was $0.12 cents. As I stood there waiting patiently for my $0.13 cents change the White lady asked "What ya waiting on boy?" and I replied "My change." She responded "I don't owe you nothing." Now I know I am not stupid or crazy but 25 minus 12 should equal 13, and I told her this. At this point things had gotten a little heated and out of the back comes her husband with a double barrel shot gun. "I know you not sassing my wife boy." The next thing I know is my father grabbing me by the neck and saying "No sir, we be on our way." and we were gone. That night the sheriff came to talk with granddad and I still think that's why we were back in Philly sooner than planned.

A year had passed it was 1962 and during that time you could receive your social security card and work permit at age 13. My father acquired me a position as paper picker at the Philadelphia Zoo where he worked in the maintenance department. It was a weekend position during school but full time in the summer. Our job is to make the zoo ready for visitors, empty all trash cans, pick paper from all lawns etc. from the day before. So we started work before visitors arrive and maintain the grounds during the day. This was a job normally held for the sons and friends of the White employees. It was only weekends, but it was a job with a pay check. I was to be part of a four man crew, two White high school football players from Jersey and one from Philly. Needless to say it was not the warmest of welcomes. They spent no time in letting me know that I was not welcome in their fraternity. Every morning we were given our assigned areas to work. I would get places like the picnic groves or the back road, not to be in the public eye as much. However, the two jocks would find their way to my area. The harassment started with them degrading my father trying to get me to fight or playing, let's play keep away with the nigga's hat. This went on every weekend and the entire summer, going to my dad was out of the question. He had caught them once, of course they lied and told him we were just playing. The following summer we were back once more and my first act was to warn them that I was not taking that shit anymore. One of them laughed and said "Little nigga what you think your going to do?" the other one responded "Nobody would believe you, plus my daddy is a director." So, it came to pass, I was frustrated and had enough and threw a punch. The next thing I knew, they had me by the ankles and I was eye to eye with a tiger. They had me dangling over the tiger's mote. As I looked in the eyes of the tiger the thoughts and feelings that went through my mine can not be put into words. The tiger and I bonded and that same hell that he was going to bring on me, I was now committed to bring to them. There was no one around and no tears, I was told " You better not say anything or the next time we drop you." I continued on with my day, my mind racing with thoughts of how do I make them pay. Guns, knives, poison all sorts of things came

to mind. But this would have to be something special. It came to me as I walked from the bus stop,as I passed the shoe repair shop. I saw the rawhide shoe laces from the window. They have whipped on me enough now it's my turn, I'll make a whip. I walked in the shop and brought four strands of five foot rawhide. Stopped at Groin's shop and asked him for some three quarter inch carpet tacks. My design was in emotion, I knew how to braid from doing my sisters' hair. My plan, to make a four foot whip with three quarter inch carpet tacks on the striking end. My brother and I worked on it over the weekend and made plans on how to conceal it and get it to work. Everything was in position. That following weekend, my plan was put in motion. We were in the locker room when they started. I drew my whip and it struck one of them across the cheek. I had become that tiger and they kept their distance from there in. Working with the public gives you insight to people and the type of society you live in. I was often called "Nigga!" by White kids through the fence while working. Sometimes just walking through the crowd you would here the word.

During the cold months when the zoo was in slow mode, I would work with my uncle on his Frank's soda truck. The manufacturing plant was in south Philly, which was basically Italian. Normally I would carpool with my uncle, there were a few times when I had to take public transportation. Standing at a bus stop in south Philly at that time was a scary ordeal. We would deliver through out the city but mainly the upper end, Olney, Frankford and Northeast. All of these areas were whites only at this time. We would bring our lunch because we were not welcome at a lot of the places we delivered to. Some places we could order, but we had to eat in the truck. During all of this Frank Rizzo and his police gang were like the Nazis in Germany when it came to Black people. They were told to harass and degrade blacks when ever possible. I remember leaving a meeting with a friend, we were working with Model City to help the community. We were standing on the corner discussing some issues, when up pull two white police officers. This was when we learned not to talk back to the police. "Up against the wall Niggas, you know what to do." Placed us in the back of the squad car and started driving. We asked "What da fuck did we do?" "You about to find out.", one officer said, they then told us to get out of the car. The next thing we heard was the loudspeaker from the squad car and the words "There's some niggas in the neighborhood." as they drove away. Lights started coming on in houses, people started coming outside, men, women, kids. They had bats, brooms, golf clubs, we looked at each other and without saying a word started running, hearts beating through our chest. Once we crossed the tracks of Girard Avenue we knew we were safe. Everyone kind of honored the across the tracks rule, none the less sometimes there would be some who broke the rule. There was such an incident when a nine year old young black boy was beaten by some whites for shinning shoes on the wrong side of the tracks. It was a stand off, whites on one side, Blacks on the other and the police in the middle.

Everyone had hope for the sixties, love, stop the war, equal rights etc. For a black man it was Jail or Vietnam, for some Canada. My father had seen to it that we had the tools necessary to get through life. He once said," Knowledge, what you got in yo head is the only thing they can't take from you." He equipped us with the World Book Encyclopedia along with the Negro Heritage Library. It was high school time and a time of awareness. I attended Benjamin Franklin High school on Broad street, which was 99% black and all male. I remember sitting in my counselor's office, she looking through my records and saying,"I see your father works at the zoo?" I replied "Yes ma'am." She went on to inform me that since my father was listed as a carpenter and maintenance person that this should also be the path for me, as she stated "You people are good with your hands." Being a black school we wondered why we couldn't get the name changed to represent those attending there along with a few courses that reflect our culture and history. As high school students we decided to take these issues to the Board of Education. We started our journey down Broad street when we were meant by Rizzo's police and a tank with the order to shot to kill if necessary. The police moved in, I looked on and my fears grew as I saw what the officers were doing to a White Priest. I thought to myself, if they do this to their own, I don't stand a chance

This was also the time of proms, I had met a beautiful young lady, named Escolita while working at the zoo. She was half German and half Cherokee and lived in Germantown where her parents owned a cleaners. She warned me that her parents thought everyone from North Philly were thugs and dope dealers. But it was required that I meet them. I will never forget walking in the cleaners and no one was at the counter. I yelled "Hello?", her mother came running out from the back holding a shotgun. She was screaming "Get out, we don't want your kind around my daughter." Her father soon followed and grabbed the weapon. To my surprise he was the same shade as me, she was a blond German with a temper. We were soon comfortable with each other after a few more visits. Now, she attended an all White Catholic high school so this was going to be an experience. As soon as we walked in all eyes were on us, people stopped talking in mid conversation. None the less I made the best of the situation.

It was 1968 I was sitting on my mother's front steps looking at the front page of the newspaper , and it read "Life expectancy of black youth in north Philly is 18 years old" I was going on 19. As I sat there thinking I received a call from one of my consolers wanting to know if I would be interested in attending a big ten school. I jumped at the chance, it seems the University of Illinois was recruiting for a program called Project 500. The goal was to get 500 black inner city kids from all around the country to enroll at this big ten college. They only colleges we knew of were our local institutions and what we may have seen on TV. For a lot of us it was our first plane ride, I worked all summer and saved for the journey. We all were to report on campus two weeks before classes for orientation. We all were housed in a fabulous dorm, complete with fireplace and swimming pool. This however was soon short lived. We were dispersed throughout the campus. I received my room assignment, which was in Snyder Hall a part of the men residence hall complex. I entered my room and there stood this white family, mom and dad had come to help their young son get settled in his room. I said "Hello, I'm Leroy McCray." the young man said" I'm Scott." The parents did not utter a word. I had an early class that morning and when I returned Scott and all his belongings were gone. The next morning when I woke and started out to the showers there was a noose hanging from my door. The beginning of my higher education. The young ladies of our group did not fair as well. It seems the university did not plan for all of us to make it. There were young ladies being housed in laundry rooms, sleeping on cots and ironing boards. We as black men offered to give up our rooms so the ladies could be comfortable. We needed to have a meeting with the Chancellor to get this accomplished. There was a meeting to be held at the student union, where we hoped to meet with the Chancellor and resolve this and some other issues on the table. We were having a peaceful sit-in, in the south lounge and waiting on the arrive of the Chancellor. Time had passed and us being new to campus had no idea of the union regulations and rules. It was past midnight, when someone noticed movement outside on the quad. The university had brought in

dogs and riot police to remove us from the union. It was at this point that a lot of us started to break off table legs and lamps to fashion something to defend ourselves. We negotiated to have the women released and were told they would be escorted back to their dorms. We later learned they were put in U-haul trucks and taken to jail. We later decided to disarm ourselves and submit peacefully. We too were taken away in u haul trucks, some went to jail others were taken to the basement of the stadium and held. The charges were later dropped with the help from the community and the University's College of Law.

I remember having to get on the work study program and them placing me at the library. The librarian's comment was " Well we can't have him out front checking out books." So they put me in the basement, gave me a feather duster, the combination to the vault and a desk with a phone. This was the vault and the archives where those working on their masters and PHD's would request material. I was to answer the phone, locate the requested material and place it on the dumb waiter along with dusting the archives. There were those who were none to pleased about 500 Black students invading the campus. I must say myself, grades were very hard to come by. I had a rhetoric professor that refused to give anything above a "C". He would also never hand you your work after grading it. I soon had enough and put white out over his grade, I then took the paper to the dean and ask that he review my paper. His grade was a "B+" I then revealed the grade I was given which was a "C-". I was even told by one professor that he did not want us at his university and this was echoed by some students as well. As stated before, we were from all parts of the country and state. Being part of the Black student organization we were obligated to help all people in need. We were called on to take part in a march in Cairo Illinois to show support for fair housing. It was a peaceful march, the white folks lined the street. I can still see this middle aged white woman stepping of the curb saying "Nigga!" as she spat on me. It took all the strength I could muster not to respond.

Being in college and away from home you are often home sick. It was the Christmas holidays and I couldn't wait to get home. Because of my family's financial situation I was unable to go home every break or holiday. I recall talking with my cousin who I missed and making it a point to see her while in Philly. She lived in west Philly and I would have to take public transportation. As I stood at the bus stop on the second leg of my travels it started snowing. As the thoughts of Christmas ran through my mind, there came a voice "Motha fucka, don't move!" I looked around and there were three police squad cars and a patty wagon, about eight police officers all with their guns drawn and at me. Luckily I had on gloves and my hands were not in my pockets. I turned to the wall as directed and was then slammed against it. I tried explaining that I was a college student just going to visit my cousin,"Store just got robbed, with someone fitting your description." one of the officers shouted. The doors of the patty wagon opened and there four other young Black men with the same attire as myself. The winter fashion of young people during this time was, blue jeans, combat boots and a pea jacket. What really amazed me was that all of us were different shades. We arrived at the location of the store and were filed out for a line up. A small Asian lady walked up and down viewing us all, there was a lump in my throat waiting on her decision. We were told we could go, I asked if we were being taken back to where we were picked up. No one said a word.

It was my junior year and I was taking an African Art History class. It was great we had worked hard to get the university to add this curriculum and I was in this class. I was seated and a little early when the instructor came in. She was a White woman wearing a Dashiki. If that wasn't bad enough she started by saying "I'm here to teach you about primitive art." From that point we were at odds all semester long.

Lady you White first of all, second you said primitive, how can you teach me about me. We bumped heads from the start. Her grading too was a little on the light side. However, me having a product design major, one of the papers I wrote was on the many contributions Africa has given to mankind. From utensils, pulley system, metal forging, furniture just to name a few. For this paper I received a "B-".

Enduring and growing, I finally graduated along with a wife and a son. Her being from Chicago and me never seeing Black people with this much space. I decided this is the place for me. My wife's mother had retired from social security and completed her dream. Her dream, to move her children out of the projects into a house. She completed his mission and acquired a home at 87th and Merrill ave. She passed away a year after. My wife and I, her being the oldest moved into the home. There was a White family living next door to us, that Saturday a U-haul truck was being loading. There were a few more families on the block that soon followed suit.

I was fresh out of college with a family and a home and no job. I soon hit the bricks running, thumbing through the want ads, not knowing the city that well I soon found myself in some strange places. I had just come from an interview and was standing at a bus stop when this school bus of White, high school, baseball team pulled up at the light. They were screaming out the window "Nigga, nigga, nigga!" two of them started to get off the bus, "We going to kill us a nigga." one said. I put down my portfolio and put my hand in my pocket grabbing my knife. One screamed again "Nigga!" and I replied "Yo mama a nigga, now if one of you want to die, come on." The bus driver yelled out to them "Take your seats." and he drove off. Soon a CTA bus pulled up the door opened and there was a Black man driving, who spoke to me with fear in his voice "Brotha, what's wrong with you don't you know were you are?" It seems I was in Marquette Park, the heart of the Klan strong hole. It was at this point that I looked around and saw the sign painted on the side of a building saying "Kill all Niggers" My heart dropped as I jumped on the bus.

My job hunting continued, the rejects were many. The demand for Black Product Designers were few if not at all in 1973. So I decided to place myself in the Draftsman arena. I procured a Draftsman position in Franklin Park Illinois. However my commute was something to be desired, the 87th street bus to the Dan Ryan el, the el to down town Chicago, a bus to Union station, a commuter train to Franklin Park then a bus to work. The associates at work were great people. I was just told the time the last train left and be cautious not to miss it. There however was one time when I was doing some overtime on a project, got to the train station and the Franklin Park Police were there waiting with me. I boarded the train and they drove away.

I continued to look for better opportunities and found myself in Skokie Illinois as a Configuration Control Administrator. One of my duties, was to make sure the production line had the correct blue prints for each station. I would hear the whispers of "Who that nigga think he is." and "He think he somebody." On occasion I would have to go to Skokie Valley Reproduction and purchase some needed supplies. A few times I was stopped by the Skokie Police with the same reasoning "There's been some burglaries in the area and we're just being cautious." or "There was a car fitting this description." Let me remind you, my job required I wear a shirt and tie, most times a sports coat. This occurred on times I was just going to lunch as well.

My wife and I were at a point of irreconcilable differences and it was time to move on. I moved in with a college friend of mine who was also from Philly. This was in Wrigleyville on the north side of the city. There were very few Blacks in the area at this time, which was around the late 70's. I remember a friend and I going into a little corner bar called Bernie's. You had to be buzzed into this place. We walked in and the bartender confronted us my saying "We don't serve niggas here." and I replied "I don't blame you, I won't serve them either. I can't stand niggas." Everyone in the place were like a deer in headlights. "I'll have a vodka and tonic and give him what he's drinking" pointing to my friend. The next thing we knew, someone was buying us drinks.

My brother, a college friend and myself lived in an apartment on Addison and Wilton avenue. We often gathered on the lake front, playing softball or just having fun. A friend and I had gotten in my car and were leaving through the alley when two White police officers pulled up in back of us. We had just pulled out of my parking space in back of the apartment. They demanded we step out of the vehicle, and we did. When asked why we were stopped. They once again responded "There has been some burglaries in the area, by some guys that fit your description." A Black guy and a short Puerto Rican, I don't think so, what are the odds. They searched us both, one officer found a joint I had in my shirt pocket and laughed, "This is great, we can have this for later." as they left laughing.

There weren't many Blacks in the area so we tended to gravitate to each other. Seems we all had children around the same age as well. Such was the relationship I had with a friend, Gary that worked as a News Editor for NBC. It was a Saturday morning and we had just gotten back from his kid's doctor appointment. Being his kid was only about 4 or 5 years old the doctor gave him a syringe with the needle missing filled with water. We dropped him off at home, not knowing that he left the syringe in the backseat. We were on the northwest side on our way to his mother's house when the police pulled us over. Two White officers a young full of energy guy and a older more seasoned gentleman. Gary was upset not knowing why we were stopped he asked the young officer "What's the problem officers? We didn't do anything." The young officer replied "That's for me to determine." The older officer had asked me to step out of the car and show him my identification. Gary was complaining to the other officer " Man, this is a bunch of hype, do you know who I work for." The officer replied " No, and I don't give a shit." As he proceeded to search the car. I kept trying to convince Gary to calm down, to no avail. Then it happened, the officer found the syringe. This made his day, "A bunch of hype hey. Get your ass against the car you're under arrest." The older officer turned to me and said "It's not your car, you can go." I felt in my heart something was wrong so I said no I'll ride to the station with my friend. His wife later came and posted bail for him.

Just when you think things can't get any worst, here it comes. My roommates and I (all from Philly) got the news the Police had bombed the MOVE house in Philly. We turned on the news and there it was. "Home" was under attack...

The 1985 MOVE bombing in Philadelphia, Pennsylvania

I soon connected with and married my childhood sweetheart, and had a daughter. Things were looking up. We lived in a one bedroom apartment on Janssen and Addison in the Wrigleyville area. We often shopped at the Jewel's grocery store about two blocks away on Southport. None the less, there came the night that will forever be etched in my mind. My wife had gone shopping as she normally would do. I did my fatherly duty and watched our daughter. Then it happened, she opened the door in tears, knees bleeding, clothes all mudded and wet,. I rushed to comfort her, when she told me what happened. Some white men in a blue pickup truck tried to run her over, calling her a Nigga bitch. She did all she could do to get out of the way as they ran over our cart of food. Upset is not the word I would use

to describe my feelings at that point. We gathered ourselves and did what we thought was the right thing, we called the police. Two White officers arrived she gave them a description of the vehicle and a partial license plate number. Their response was, "Thank you we'll look into it." It was at that point I realized they were not going to do anything. It was time to take it to the street. My only thought was finding these two animals. I grabbed my gun and put myself in hunting mode. I walked down to were my wife told me this happened, there was my food and cart, laying in the rain in the middle of the street. Mr. D the owner of D'Agostino's restaurant and friend of the family saw me and he saw something he had never seen before. The first thing he said was "Give me the gun." He saw it in my eyes. He told me to go home and take care of my family, I did.

Our daughter was growing at what seemed to be rapid speed and my son also wanted to come live with us. We soon moved to a larger apartment located near Byron and Clark streets. I finally started a part time position as a product designer at a major power tool manufacture, also located in Skokie. They kept me as a part time employee for two and a half years before I became a full time associate. Upon getting the position there was an increase in salary even though I was part time. My father once told me, given the chance to purchase myself a good pair of shoes. This was my chance, I had been eying these Stacy Adams $175.00 for a while but they were out of my reach at the time. This was my day,cash money in my pocket and all my bills paid. As soon as I walked in the door I was greeted by this white sales guy. "Can I help you?" he said and I replied "I'd like to see the Stacy's in the window in a 91/2 maroon please." His whole demeanor was wrong, he responded " No problem, you know they're $175 but we have a great layaway plan." How dear you assume anything about me, were my thoughts. He indicated he would have to get them from the back. There was another salesperson standing by and I could see his facial response when his associate made the remarks about cost and layaway. I immediately asked for his help. The salesman returned and was surprised, I cleared the air for him. "Thanks, but I think I would rather have him waiting on me. I want him to get the commission." I then proceeded to buy socks, shoe polish, extra shoe strings and paid cash. It was worth the look on his face.

The neighborhood was great, accept when there was a Cubs game. The parking became unbearable along with the crowd. However, when the game is in progress all is quiet only the cheers from the ballpark get your attention. It was during this quiet time that I allowed my little girl outside to ride her bike. As I sat on our steps watching her be happy riding up and down the sidewalk thinking about how great life can be, the game was over and the crowd began to flow.

Some were nice and then there were the three white men I saw push my child out of the way saying " You little niggers don't belong here." as they laughed. I was horrified and outraged at the same time, " Motha fucka touch her again and I'll kill you!" I yelled as I stood up on our top step. They approached but not coming up the steps. "Bring your ass down here nigger and see what happens." It was at this point that my wife came outside and placed my gun in my hand, but doing it so as not to let them know. She then got my daughter to come in the house leaving the bike on the grass. "No, it's three of you motha's bring yo ass up my steps." They must have come to their senses or was it the look in my eyes and the tone in my voice, because there was nothing else said and they backed off and continued down the street. I hadn't even showed them my gun, which wouldn't have fired anyway the trigger was broken.

Like most working couples Saturday was our shopping day. We tried to get it done as early as possible. This Saturday proved to be a little different however. We were going up and down the isles, fussing at our daughter as we went. Her wanting everything she had seen on TV. She ran up ahead of us and crossed paths with an elderly couple who were doing their shopping as well. Which was a great scene, small child and an elderly couple. But then it came, the words "Damn, little Niggers everywhere, get the hell out the way." was his spoiler for that moment. My wife turned to me, "Don't say nothing." were her words and I calmed myself and we kept moving.

Things were going great at the job in my eyes. It was however going on two and a half years and I was still temporary. The company was in the process of merging with a company based in Germany. It was during a meeting with the Director of Engineering that I was recognized and hired full time for the design work I had achieved regarding the German brand product. We were then told we would have to take some classes on German sensitivity, German culture and how to deal with Germans. This however did not upset me. What did, was being friends with the Executive Secretary to the President of the company who informs you that the wife of the President of the company was told, if she wanted to visit the south side of Chicago as she requested she would need to get some shots. I am still trying to digest this, can someone enlighten me please.

Wrigleyville was starting to change, more bars and people started cropping up in the neighborhood. Just so happened, I had a cousin who was working for AMTRAK and was looking for property in Chicago, were he was based. However the ironic part was, he had to pretend to be Jamaican in order to acquire the corner lot two flat four unit building on Logan Boulevard he so badly wanted. It's funny how you are looked at with different eyes if you're not African American. Upon finalizing the sale he requested that my wife and I move in and help manage the building when he's on the road. His run was from Chicago to Seattle Washington which meant he was on the road for three days and off for three. The wife and I agreed and we took the large apartment on the first floor front. Above us was an elderly couple, he was a retired Chicago police officer who hated Black people. But as karma would have it he was suffering from dementia and a stroke. His wife was getting on in age and would often bang on the floor when she needed help, usually getting him in and out of bed or when he's fallen trying to do for himself. I still remember the hatred in his eyes when I first picked him up from the floor. This would continue for more than three years.

My son was now in high school and into the $200 Micheal Jordan stage. So, I got him a job at the nearest Jewels Osco. He was enjoying his job, saving money and the manager loved him. Months had gone by when I noticed a change in him, we talked and my heart dried as he informed me of what the issue was. It seems, he was helping a woman(White) with her groceries and was confronted by her boyfriend/ husband and informed that if he ever walk with her again he was going to kill him. He was seventeen years old trying to be helpful. He goes on to become a manager of a Family Dollar store and gets pulled over in Indiana, in a company van for what the White officer said was speeding. Doing 50mph in a 45mph zone. Which upon appearing in court was found to be the M.O.(targeting Blacks) of this officer and was thrown out by the court.

Cancer is probably the worst word anyone can hear. I had opted for the surgery and was in the stage of recovery at home. It was during this time the director of H.R. gave me a call. He informed me that the company had eliminated my position and my services were no longer needed. Some days later I received a call from an associate at the company informing me that they had promoted an associate a White immigrant that I had helped train, into the same position I had with a different title. My first thought was, the hell with them. But I soon gathered myself and contacted EEOC (Equal Employment Opportunity Commission). They informed me that, it was illegal for HR to contact me while on medical leave and also to dismiss me as they did. I in turn put through the paper work for a lawsuit. After receiving the notification of a lawsuit, I was contacted and asked when would I be available to come back to work and discuss where we go from here. I was soon reinstated and the suit was dropped.

A lot of U.S companies started to move the production overseas to China. There was an exchange of personnel as well. We were again informed we would need to take sensitivity training. It was at this point I realized, no one has offered Black sensitivity training. Things had gotten to the point were I was overseeing or apart of projects and traveling to different manufacturing facilities. I remember my first trip to the manufacturing plant in New Bern North Carolina. I was the only Black in our group. When we walked in the restaurant and everything stopped, all eyes turned to me. I looked down to see if my fly was open or something. When it hit me, I was Black in their restaurant.

Things happen at strange times in life. The head of security at corporate headquarter was a Black man and a friend. He had just passed his thirty second degree as a Mason. We took pictures in front of my house to celebrate. He was very proud of what he had accomplished and brought the photos to work to share. My director saw these photos and asked "Leroy is this your house?" I replied "Yes." The next thing that came out of his mouth surprised me to no end. He said, " You have grass." I wanted to respond with "I also have a lawnmower." but I didn't.

My travel times became more frequent. Walnut Ridge Arkansas, population in the year 2000, 97.04% white, 0.59% Black, 0.51% Native American,0.12% Asian, and 1.75% from two or more races. 0.43% of the population were Hispanic or Latino of any race.I remember going there with other engineers (White engineers) and things were always fine. I was preparing for a trip to Walnut with only one other person when the head of security informed me that he had to inform Walnut Ridge's law enforcement that I was coming, this was for my safe guard. He said he constantly has to inform them when a Black person is coming down there. We arrived at the motel and checked in, I was given a room on the third floor over looking the parking lot. I settled in and ordered room service. Dinner came and it was a great meal, afterwards I walked out on the balcony just to catch some air. At that point this pickup truck pulls into the parking lot playing load country music, the Confederate flag which is also the symbol of racism, was proudly displayed in the rear window. I then heard this voice, "Is there a Nigger in town?". By this time I was in my room locking the door and

grabbing the knife from my dinner plate. Nothing else was said however the music kept playing for a few hours and then it was quiet. Morning came and we met in the lobby of the motel for breakfast then continued to the plant. Once at the plant I met the only Black man working there. He was outside inspecting his bicycle, it seems he whines up with a flat every day. He told me it was their (Whites) way of telling him he doesn't belong there. He said he didn't fear for his life and they were not running him away. I was proud.

These incidences by no means negate the countless number of times being followed by security in a grocery or department store or the White lady that grabs her purse on the elevator. They are just a look, maybe at yourself or a look at what we call "The land of the Free." If we are to change and be a nation of one people, land of the free and home of the brave we need to start first by taking a note from a Micheal Jackson song....Start with the man in the mirror.

We have fallen short as a society and a country for letting

Hollywood, large Corporations, politicians and the media control our history. In todays world of instant information the true history is there we just have to correct our history books and our way of thinking and teachings. We need to correct all the falsehoods that have been and are still being taught. For generations we have taught about Christopher Columbus discovering America and we celebrate Columbus Day. But who was Amerigo Vespucci and why isn't this country called Columbus?

From Wikipedia, the free encyclopedia
Stockholm syndrome is a condition in which hostages develop a psychological alliance with their captors during captivity. Emotional bonds may be formed between captors and captives, during intimate time together, but these are generally considered irrational in light of the danger or risk endured by the victims.
This term was first used by the media in 1973 when four hostages were taken during a bank robbery in Stockholm, Sweden. The hostages defended their captors after being released and would not agree to testify in court against them. It was noted that in this case, however, the police were perceived to have acted with little care for the hostages' safety, providing an alternative reason for their unwillingness to testify. Stockholm syndrome is paradoxical because the sympathetic sentiments that captives feel towards their captors are the opposite of the fear and disdain which an onlooker might feel towards the captors.

There are four key components that characterize Stockholm syndrome:
- A hostage's development of positive feelings towards the captor
- No previous relationship between hostage and captor
- A refusal by hostages to cooperate with police forces and other government authorities (unless the captors themselves happen to be members of police forces or government authorities).
- A hostage's belief in the humanity of the captor because they cease to perceive the captor as a threat when the victim holds the same values as the aggressor.

We as African Americans suffer from what I believe is "Generational Stockholm Syndrome". We have pickup and in most cases forced into the life of emulating our captors. Any effort to embrace or cultivate our own history and culture seems to always be met with resistance of some sort. The Tulsa Race Massacre in 1921 was the first aerial assault on U.S. soil. While all other Ethnic groups are uplifted. The understanding should be that we all are Ethnic groups in America. The only true Americans are the indigenous peoples of the Americas.

2020

8:46

I am an invisible man. No, I am not a spook like those who haunted Edgar Allan Poe; nor am I one of your Hollywood-movie ectoplasm. I am a man of substance, of flesh and bone, fiber and liquids -- and I might even be said to possess a mind. I am invisible, understand, simply because people refuse to see me. Like the bodiless heads you see sometimes in circus sideshows, it is as though I have been surrounded by mirrors of hard, distorting glass. When they approach me they see only my surroundings, themselves, or figments of their imagination -- indeed, everything and anything except me. Nor is my invisibility exactly a matter of a bio-chemical accident to my epidermis. That invisibility to which I refer occurs because of a peculiar disposition of the eyes of those with whom I come in contact. A matter of the construction of their inner eyes, those eyes with which they look through their physical eyes upon reality. I am not complaining, nor am I protesting either. It is sometimes advantageous to be unseen, although it is most often rather wearing on the nerves. Then too, you're constantly being bumped against by those of poor vision. Or again, you often doubt if you really exist. You wonder whether you aren't simply a phantom in other people's minds. Say, a figure in a nightmare which the sleeper tries with all his strength to destroy. It's when you feel like this that, out of resentment, you begin to bump people back. And, let me confess, you feel that way most of the time. You ache with the need to convince yourself that you do exist in the real world, that you're a part of all the sound and anguish, and you strike out with your fists, you curse and you swear to make them recognize you. And, alas, it's seldom successful. One night I accidentally bumped into a man, and perhaps because of the near darkness he saw me and called me an insulting name. I sprang at him, seized his coat lapels and demanded that he apologize. He was a tall blond man, and as my face came close to his he looked insolently out of his blue eyes and cursed me, his breath hot in my face as he struggled. I pulled his chin down sharp upon the crown of my head, butting him as I had seen the

West Indians do, and I felt his flesh tear and the blood gush out, and I yelled, "Apologize! Apologize!" But he continued to curse and struggle, and I butted him again and again until he went down heavily, on his knees, profusely bleeding. I kicked him repeatedly, in a frenzy because he still uttered insults though his lips were frothy with blood. Oh yes, I kicked him! And in my outrage I got out my knife and prepared to slit his throat, right there beneath the lamplight in the deserted street, holding him by the collar with one hand, and opening the knife with my teeth -- when it occurred to me that the man had not seen me, actually; that he, as far as he knew, was in the midst of a walking nightmare! And I stopped the blade, slicing the air as I pushed him away, letting him fall back to the street. I stared at him hard as the lights of a car stabbed through the darkness. He lay there, moaning on the asphalt; a man almost killed by a phantom. It unnerved me. I was both disgusted and ashamed. I was like a drunken man myself, wavering about on weakened legs. Then I was amused. Something in this man's thick head had sprung out and beaten him within an inch of his life. I began to laugh at this crazy discovery. Would he have awakened at the point of death? Would Death himself have freed him for wakeful living? But I didn't linger. I ran away into the dark, laughing so hard I feared I might rupture myself. The next day I saw his picture in the Daily News, beneath a caption stating that he had been "mugged." Poor fool, poor blind fool, I thought with sincere compassion, mugged by an invisible man!

By Ralph Ellison

Black Lives Matter

In My Shoes

www.ingramcontent.com/pod-product-compliance
Lightning Source LLC
Chambersburg PA
CBRC101157280526
45792CB00009B/2326